Crystals

Crystal Healing for Beginners, Discover the Healing Power of Crystals and Minerals

Faye Froome

Faye Froome Copyright © 2016

Contents

Introduction

I would like to thank you for buying my book, **"Crystals : Crystal Healing for Beginners, Discover the Healing Power of Crystals and Minerals"**

This book contains all the information you will need to learn the different healing properties of many crystals and minerals and how to apply them to gain the best results to heal yourself using the natural energies held within the crystals.

You will discover the secrets of how to cleanse your stones and crystals of negative energies, how to energize them and also how to program individual stones to aid the natural energy of your body to help you heal.

Information is also included about the seven main chakras within the body and how they are directly linked to our physical and mental wellbeing and how using crystals in alliance with your chakras can help to improve your emotional states.

Thanks again for buying this book, I hope you enjoy it!

Chapter 1 – How Crystal & Mineral Energy Works

There is much more to a crystal or a mineral stone than something attractive that we can utilize for monetary gain. Whether as a source of fuel, a beautiful piece of jewelry or a pretty stone used to decorate the home or garden, the essence of these items are 100% natural, made by nature in the same way that you and I are.

These stones have taken decades or longer to form in the depths of the Earth and during that time they have absorbed the universal energy from around them. This energy is part of, and contained within, everything within the universe and connects each individual thing to all others, including humans.

As physical entities, humans use the five senses to see, hear, taste, smell and feel things but within the physical body our spirit is housed. It is the spirit that senses things which we can't physically see or hear. It is that part of us that our intuition comes from, the part that warns us of danger and the part that connects us to the universe as a whole. The Spirit is pure, unadulterated energy and is referenced in the histories of all cultures. Referred to in a variety of ways such as chi, prana, life force, our ancient ancestors relied more on the spirit than on our physical and mental being and believed that through the energy of spirit we can touch, feel and influence the other universal energies contained in all natural things.

Everything from trees and other plants, rocks, water, the air and fire contain varying levels of this universal energy and along with their natural properties they can be used to affect our own natural energy and through this, influence the health and wellbeing of our bodies and minds.

To understand this better spend a little time holding natural items in your hands and feel their energies. Place your hand on a tree or pick up a crystal and relax, close your eyes and focus on what you are touching. If your mind is quiet enough you will notice a throbbing, tingling or vibration from it. This is the universal energy contained within it. Try this with your own energies, see if you can quiet your mind and relax, then focus on your breathing and feel your hands begin to tingle or vibrate. Don't worry if you can't open your mind enough yet, there is a later chapter which explains your body's main energy points along with information which will help you to quiet your mind enough to feel your energy.

Energy levels vary in all things and crystals and minerals are no exception. Some will contain strong levels of energy that can easily be felt with little effort while others contain only small amounts. Crystals, along with all other natural things contain properties which can heal our physical bodies, mental processes and emotional stability. Herbs are obvious as we can ingest them but with crystals and minerals the healing is more subtle.

Each type of stone has attributes which connect it to specific areas of the body and mind, and when joined with our own energies they can be directed and aid in bringing about the necessary energy balance and flow to heal physical, emotional and/or mental problems. Erratic energy flow through the body is the cause of many ailments and by bringing the necessary balance back to our body we can often heal many minor, and some major issues.

So many long term illnesses are a combination of symptoms which relate to many areas of the body. This is because a disruption in one area triggers disruptions in the energies from other areas and very quickly we present a cluster of symptoms which, when experienced together, can leave us feeling mentally or physically ill. The vibrations of pure universal energy which is contained within a crystal or mineral can influence our own energies to such a degree that the balance is brought back to the body and many of the symptoms you were experiencing will dissipate.

Energy healing works using the frequencies of the energy stored within the crystals and minerals. Everything we see, hear and feel is a combination of vibrating energy and how we recognize it depends of the frequency, (speed/strength) of the vibrations. The human body receives and translates these vibrations in a way our own energy can understand and utilize it by allowing the external energy to infiltrate our own and feed into it.

The way a crystal or mineral is formed impacts the stones ability to hold onto its energy and store it by trapping it within the layers. In some stones this can be in the form of small pockets that have formed over time within the stone causing a high concentration of energy. These pockets can contain enough electrically charged energy that they are able to alter the energies of other natural things and impact on how they grow or form. This level of energy applied to our own life force can have a highly beneficial effect on our health.

The good news is that it takes no special talents or years of dedicated learning to be able to use crystals and minerals to benefit your well being. If you intend to use crystal healing on a regular basis then learning about the healing properties of different stones is useful along with learning how to direct the energies for specific treatment, but other than that no in depth learning is necessary, although the more you know and understand, the more effective your treatments will be. A stone can have an impact just by being close to you without you even realizing it.

Chapter 2 – Preparing Your Crystals & Minerals

When our energy fields come into contact with another person's energy, we become aware of them. Even if our eyes are closed and they are silent and still, we can feel their presence. This is because both lots of energies are touching and interacting. If the other person is feeling a particular strong emotion, often we ourselves will feel some level of that same emotion because we are absorbing the energy of the other person. This is the same with the energies contained within crystals and minerals; they absorb the energy of the things around them, including peoples.

This pure energy remains within the crystal and if they are being used for healing, it is advisable to cleanse them regularly. There is negative and positive energy and you do not want negative energies entering your field, especially when healing. How often you cleanse your stones depends on how regularly they are used. If you are using them on yourself only then daily use requires once a week cleansing. Adjust this according to how often you are healing.

If stones are used on others then always cleanse after each use. You do not want to be putting another person's negative energies into someone else. If you choose not to use your crystals or minerals for direct healing, instead preferring to just keep them in a room on display, then you can cleanse them on a monthly or even bi-monthly basis to ensure you keep them free of negativity and get the most benefit from them.

Cleansing your stones is not about removing surface dirt or dust from them, it is about removing the additional energies stored within and leaving them with only their natural energy. As the natural energies are obtained from the earth as they grow, this is pure universal energy and will have only beneficial effects.

Cleansing

Salt is the most effective way to cleanse your stones but the composition of crystals and minerals varies, and as some are porous they can be damaged when they come into contact with salt. This is because salt itself is a crystalline material and when it is absorbed into a salt based crystal the entire make-up of the stone can be altered. Additionally, if your stone contains water or any type of metal, salt will damage it so if you choose this method of cleansing you should be certain that you understand the nature of your stones.

Never allow any of the following stones to be cleansed using a salt water mix.

- Turquoise
- Tourmaline
- Topaz
- Tigers Eye
- Tanzanite
- Selenite
- Sapphire
- Ruby
- Pyrite
- Opal
- Moonstone
- Malachite
- Lapis Lazuli
- Jet
- Hematite
- Halite
- Gypsum
- Garnet
- Emerald
- Calcite
- Beryl
- Azurite

There are five ways which you can cleanse your crystals and minerals:

1. Salt Water Cleanse

2. Geodes

3. Contact Salt

4. Non-Contact Salt

5. Smudging

Salt Water
Initial Cleansing: 5 – 7 days
Maintenance Cleansing: 12 – 24 hours

1. Fill a plastic or glass bowl with cool, boiled water and stir in a good amount of salt.

2. Place crystals or minerals into the salted water. Ensure they are fully submerged and leave for the required time.

3. Remove stone and rinse will warm water to ensure no salt is left coating the stone.

Geodes
Initial Cleansing: 3 – 5 days
Maintenance Cleansing: 1 – 3 days

A Quartz Geode Cave is one of the best ways to cleanse your crystals as quartz will absorb all energy from the crystals or mineral's, neutralize it then return the pure energy back into your stone. Simply place your stones within the cave and leave them.

Geode caves can be costly but you will only need one to cleanse all your stones, and as there is a large variety of types of quartz crystal, the price can be reasonable depending on the variety of quartz you choose.

Best Types of Quartz Geodes

- Amethyst
- Ametrine
- Aventurine
- Blue Quartz
- Citrine
- Milky Quartz
- Rock Crystal
- Rose Quartz
- Smoky Quartz
- Tigers Eye

Contact Salt
Initial Cleansing: 5 – 7 days
Maintenance Cleansing: 12 – 24 hours
1. Use a plastic or glass bowl and quarter fill it with salt. (General household salt is fine but sea salt is better)

2. Place your stones into the salt then fill up the bowl until the stones are fully covered

3. Rinse with warm water to remove any salt residue

Non-Contact Salt
Initial Cleansing: 1 week
Maintenance Cleansing: 2 – 4 days
1. Fill a bowl or deep tray with salt

2. Take a smaller container and place your crystals into it

3. Place the smaller container into the salt. The smaller bowl containing your crystals or minerals should be sunk into the salt until it reaches two thirds up the sides)

Smudging
Initial Cleansing: 5 minutes
Maintenance Cleansing: 1 – 2 minutes
Smudging involves holding your crystals in the smoke from either a smudging stick or an incense stick or cone. The smoke removes all stored additional energies from the crystal leaving it filled with only pure energy.

For cleansing use only Sage, Sandalwood or Cedarwood incenses.
1. Light the incense and, when burning well, place the crystal or mineral into the smoke and hold it there so it becomes engulfed in the smoke.

Crystal Energizing

Unless you are using a Geode Cave to cleanse your stones, all crystals and minerals will need to be re-energized so they can be used to good effect. There are four ways this can be done and all are highly effective so you should choose whichever way you feel best suits you.

Energizing can be done using:

- Personal Contact

- Natural Light

- Water

- Geode Cave

Personal Contact

Throughout the world there are a several cultures who maintain that the best way to re-energize a healing stone is through personal contact. While this does work, I personally feel that the act of infusing the stone with the energy of someone who may be ill or emotionally charged will negate the effects of cleansing it, but this is a matter of personal choice.

- Cup your crystal or mineral in your hands and hold if for 30 minutes to 1 hour.

Natural Light

If you are using stones that are deeply colored, direct sunlight may cause them to fade a little.

The natural energy of the sun or moon is a good way to re-energize your stones.

- Place your crystals and minerals onto a clean surface outdoors. (I find placing them into a candle holder that can be hung from a tree branch works well)

- Leave them outdoors to absorb the energy from the natural light for 1 – 2 days.

Water

If you have access to a river or other free running natural water source, then take advantage of it as this is the most effective and fastest way to re-energize a stone. Running water is the quickest and easiest way to re-energies a stone. **This must never be done with any stones which are porous.**

- Natural Running Water: Place your stones into a bag made from natural materials and hold it in the stream or river for 5 minutes

- Tap Water: Place your stones into an open topped containing and place under a running tap for 15 to 20 minutes

Geode Cave

- As with the cleansing, simply place your stones into a Geode Cave and leave for at least 24 hours

Chapter 3 – Healing With Stones

There is no one way in which to use crystals and minerals to the best effect. It is down to the severity of the illness and the personal judgment of whoever is guiding or using the stones. Each natural substance has a variety of uses which can affect the mental, emotional, physical and spiritual elements that make up a human being.

Stones can be placed close to or onto the body, using chakra points or simply placing them close to your skin; they may be placed around you or used as a tool of focus and guidance when meditating. The proximity of the crystal or mineral to the skin directly effects the concentration of the energy so if only a subtle healing is required then it is entirely possible for someone to benefit from the stones without even realizing it is happening.

Before you begin to use a healing stone you should consider all the options and decide personally which type of healing is required and how it will be obtained based solely on the condition(s) being treated at that time.

Some highly effective techniques are listed below with full instructions following of any practices involved with the treatment:

Jewelry

Jewelry is an excellent way to ensure a stone is kept in close contact to the person who requires treatment. Whether it is in the form of a bracelet, necklace, earrings or a ring, the closer the stone to the skin, the more effective it will be. This technique is best suited to long term, ongoing treatment but it is important to ensure that the stone is cleansed regularly.

To gain a higher level of benefit, if the jewelry is situated close to or on a chakra point which corresponds to the affected area, (see following chapter for information on chakra points), then the energies will be directed to the desired area in a much stronger way, gaining a better result. Additionally, any area's which correspond with the stone itself, and that are not governed by that particular chakra, will still be stimulated and healed.

If you make your own jewelry then let your inner spirit choose the stone for you where possible. This is easier if you have a selection of the same stones. While every one of the stones will be helpful in your healing, if your sub-conscious, (spirit), chooses it then the healing benefits will be increased.

Body contact

Jewelry is not the only way a stone can be carried with you. Even something as simple as placing a stone in your jacket pocket will promote healing energy. You could choose to carry a small bag of stones, place one in your purse/wallet or a pocket or even attach them to clothing or your mobile phone. The closer it is to you, the stronger the impact but so long as it is close by you then you will reap the rewards of it energy,

Sleep & Environment

Placing crystals or minerals around your home will provide a constant, subtle healing energy. It will not be as effective as skin contact but even a crystal in the same room as you will provide a therapeutic benefit.

Consider where you are placing your stone and what you wish to achieve, for example, if you struggle to sleep at night, place stones with sleep inducing or anxiety relieving properties on your nightstand or beneath your pillow. If you struggle will concentration and or motivation, place one on your desk or close to you at your place of work. Symptoms of depression can also be relieved by keeping relevant crystals around your home.

Bathing

This may seem like a strange way to use crystal healing but try adding non-porous stones to your bath water or around your bathroom when you bathe.

Crystals and minerals are spiritually and emotionally cleansing, and when bathing we are generally in a relaxed state so a crystal bath can be highly effective. If placed into your bath water the healing energies and absorbed into the water giving an extra boost to their natural properties.

Meditating

Many crystals and mineral have naturally relaxing and calming properties in addition to the active healing energy they contain so using a stone while meditating can aid healing. As meditation involves opening up and connecting with your spirit, this boosts the effectiveness of the stones because your energy channels are already open and flowing well.

Holding or focusing on a stone during a meditation will allow you to better guide the stones energy and, if you wish to take it one step further, you can use the meditation as an opportunity to charge the crystal with your own energy, strengthening the link and strengthening the focus of healing. If you later carry this stone with you then the effects on your ailments will increase in intensity, helping you to heal faster.

Chakra Healing

Placing the correct/corresponding stones on top of your chakra points will help with channeling the stones energy into the areas of your body which require the most healing. This will allow you to channel intense rivers of energy directly to the affected area and focus the crystals energy onto a specific point.

To gain the best results from chakra healing you should open your chakras, ensure they are free from blockages and spend a minimum of 10 minutes in a meditative state while the crystal(s) is placed on the correct chakra(s). Depending on the nature of the illness, you may need to do this on a daily basis for a short while.

Chapter 4 – The Chakra's

A chakra is an energy centre within the body, a place where we can access the universal energy which makes up our life force. Our bodies contain many chakra points but the seven main ones are the ones you will mostly use when performing crystal healing. They are situated in a vertical line from your pelvis to the crown of your head, and each main chakra has branches coming from it which reach to other parts of the body.

When the main chakra points are unblocked, the energy flows in a free and balanced way throughout your entire body. When this flow becomes unstable, whether through blockages or because we are allowing it to surge through us far too fast, the effects are felt within our body and mind and can lead to health issues, mental disturbance, emotional unbalance and a general feeling of illness and lethargy.

The main chakras each relate to different physical and mental areas of the body, and using relevant crystals or minerals, in combination with a stable chakra system, can present amazing results.

All chakra points have associated stones but in the absence of the correct stones, a clear quartz crystal is highly effective for all chakra points.

Root Chakra

Associated Color: Red

Associated Crystals & Minerals: All Red or Black Stones can be used when working with the root chakra

- Black Tourmaline
- Fire Agate
- Garnet
- Hematite
- Red Aventurine
- Rhodonite
- Ruby
- Smoky Quartz

Chakra One is the Root Chakra, located in the pelvic area.
It controls your physical energy, all physical functions such as movement and is responsible for the fight or flight reflex and all elements relating to self preservation and the survival instinct. Psychologically, this is the chakra used to ground ourselves and balances mental illnesses.

In addition to the above, the root chakra is responsible for all things connected to the adrenal glands which produce hormones and any issues regarding fertility can be addressed through this chakra point. Ailments related to the spine are also channeled through this energy centre along with bladder, prostrate and kidney problems.

On a psychological, mental and emotional level, this chakra can be worked on to ease aggressive behavior directed towards yourself or other, lack of sex drive and impotency problems, panic and anxiety issues along with hypertension, depressive moods or depressive illness, agoraphobia, eating disorders and lowered self confidence and self esteem.

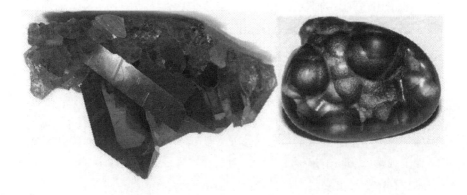

Smoky Quartz & Fire Agate

Sacral Chakra

Associated Color: Orange

Associated Crystals & Minerals: All Orange Stones can be used when working with the sacral chakra along with blue/green stones

- Adamite
- Blue Turquoise
- Blue Fluorite
- Emerald
- Moss Agate
- Orange Calcite
- Carnelian

Chakra Two is the Sacral Chakra, located in the womb area (between pelvis and navel)

This chakra controls all elements of pleasure and creative thought and expression. As this is the pleasure centre of your life energy it affects all elements concerning reproduction and sex drive. Many of the areas covered by this chakra also relate to the root chakra, and if both become blocked the impact will severely impair the common areas.

This chakra also impacts on the legs, urinary system and bowel. When blocked problems such as hormonal imbalance can occur leading to a variety of symptoms, the most severe of which is infertility. Sexual energy is depleted and problems with the kidneys and urination may occur along with disruptions to the bowel and back problems.

Because of its link to creativity, imagination and pleasure, a blogged or clogged sacral chakra can cause issues mentally, psychologically and emotionally with symptoms presenting as addictive behaviors, dependency, depression and irrationality.

Orange Calcite & Unpolished Moss Agate

Solar Plexus Chakra

Associated Color: Yellow

Associated Crystals & Minerals: All yellow or gold stones can be used to work with the solar plexus chakra

- Citrine
- Golden Labradorite
- Jasper (yellow)
- Topaz (yellow)
- Pyrite
- Tigers Eye

Chakra Three is the Solar Plexus Chakra, located at the navel area.

This is an important chakra as it is linked to our sense of self and intelligence. It helps to regulate the thought process, promotes a confidence in who we are and what we want to do and be and balances our level of self control.

On a physical level this energy centre is linked to the stomach, all bladder and pancreas and as such it can aid in the balanced production of insulin and help keep digestive upsets at bay. It is also responsible for the liver.

A blockage or clogging of the sacral chakra can lead to issues concerning weight, digestion, stomach ulcers, nerve pain and respiratory and diabetic problems. Psychologically, an unbalanced energy flow in this chakra leads to insecurities and a lowering of belief in self which increasing anxiety and often results in controlling behavioral traits manifesting.

Golden Labradorite & Tigers Eye

Heart Chakra

Associated Color: Green

Associated Crystals & Minerals: All green or pink stones can be used when working with the heart chakra

- Chrysoberyl
- Green Garnet
- Jade
- Malachite
- Pink Tourmaline
- Rose Quartz

Chakra Four is the Heart Chakra, located in the centre of the chest, to the right of the heart

The Heart Chakra is the access point to our inner self, our true being. It is the centre of all feeling related to love, both of yourself and others and directly affects our emotional state and reactions. All things relating to happiness, inner calm and the ability to both feel and show empathy and compassion for others comes through the heart chakra.

Because of its association to the emotions, when this chakras energy is not free flowing, feelings of anxiety in social situations will arise, a distrust of others motives and true feelings arises and we become judgmental and even slightly paranoid. Isolation begins to look more and more appealing as time goes and the thought processes become confused.

Physically, the heart chakra is linked to the liver, lungs and heart along with the circulatory system. It is also responsible for the circulation, the heart, lungs and the liver and physical problems often manifest in these areas along with respiratory problems and panic or anxiety attacks.-

Green Garnet & Rose Quartz

Throat Chakra

Associated Color: Blue

Associated Crystals & Minerals: All blue stones can be used when working with the throat chakra

- Aquamarine
- Blue Beryl
- Blue Calcite
- Blue Topaz
- Blue Tourmaline
- Sapphire
- Turquoise

Chakra Five is the Throat Chakra, located at the throat

The throat chakra is the centre of communication, self expression, honesty and integrity, intelligent thought and intellectual ability.

Because of the link to intellect and communication, this chakra, when blocked, can seriously interfere with the ability to interact on all levels and cause confused thoughts which lead to erratic behavior which will become increasingly unstable.

Physically, the throat chakra controls the thyroid gland, upper arms, throat and lungs and the digestive processes. If it becomes blocked or clogged symptoms that may develop include pain in the head and neck, throat problems such as laryngitis and infections, thyroid disruption and gum disease.

Turquoise & Blue Tourmaline

Third Eye Chakra

Associated Color: Indigo
Associated Crystals & Minerals: All indigo and purple stones can be used to work on the third eye chakra

- Amethyst
- Azurite
- Charoite
- Flourite (purple)
- Lapis Lazuli
- Sodalite

Chakra Six is the Third Eye Chakra, located between the eyebrows

This chakra is the gateway to the imagination and spiritual vision and expression. It holds the key to our psychic abilities and ensuring it is unblocked is paramount to spiritual development.

On a psychological level, because of its connection to our spirit, when blocked this chakra causes problems to develop relating to anxiety and nervous disorders, depression, paranoia and delusional thought processes.

Physically, the third eye chakra is linked with the spinal column, ears, nose and left eye, pituitary glands and the lower brain. People who regularly suffer from sinus issues or migraines are likely to have a blocked third eye chakra. Additional physical problems relating to this energy centre is sciatica, deteriorating vision and even seizures.

Charoite & Lapis Lazuli

Crown Chakra

Associated Color: Purple or White

Associated Crystals & Minerals: All purple or white stones can be used when working with the crown chakra

- Alexandrite
- Amethyst
- Jade (purple)
- Moonstone
- Opal
- White Calcite

Chakra Seven is the Crown Chakra, located just inside the skull at the top of the head, close to the Pineal Gland

The crown chakra provides access to the core of our inner being, our soul. Through the crown we can access all the wisdom we possess without being hindered by the physical function of thought. On a physical level this chakra governs the pineal gland, right eye and upper brain.

When this chakra becomes clogged or blocked we lose the connection to our higher self, causing us to disconnect in a physical, mental, emotional and spiritual way with other people and life. We retreat into periods of isolation and shun others because we can make no sense of them. This is because we have no connection to ourselves.

This disconnection causes delusional thoughts, confusion, a lack of inner strength, sleep problems, headaches, depression and anxiety related issues. We become needy and dependent on others because we are searching for a way to connect, but ultimately, this leads to a deeper feeling of being misunderstood and causes us to disconnect further from social situations.

Moonstone & Amethyst

Chapter 5 – Healing Properties of Crystals & Minerals

Agate

Agate is a variety of chalcedony which is, in most cases, formed in areas of volcanic activity. There is a wide variety of different types of agate available in an array of colors, many of which contain some form of banding which runs throughout the stone, although some contain natural patterning which is similar to varying forms of vegetation.

In general, agate can be used to create calm within and settle fears and anxiety. It is also a beneficial stone when confidence and inner strength needs to be increased. Agate, in all its forms aids in the stimulation of imagination, creative processes and intelligent thought.

- Each variety of agate possesses its individual healing properties in addition to the above

Amazonite
- Development of psychic ability, creative processes, intellect & intuition
- Balancing of self esteem and self belief
- Strengthens communication, inner strength, honesty & commitment
- Calming enhanced emotional states
- Eases all conditions which stem from nerves and anxiety
- Aids in removing symptoms which have developed from stress conditions such as heart palpitations and breathlessness.
- Heals and/or strengthens bones, nails, teeth and hair

Amber
Although amber is not officially a crystal or mineral, (it is pine tree sap that has been petrified and is often centuries old at least), it has many healing qualities and can be used in the same way as a stone. Quite often amber contains fossilized leaves, flowers, insects and other natural deposits than has become trapped in the sap.

Amber has many uses in healing and is a great all round stone. It has the ability to absorb any and all diseased energy from the body, to help neutralize pain and settle a disturbed mind.

From the strengthening of the muscles in the brain and mucus producing muscles to enhancing the memory and aiding in the control and development of emotional control and intellect, amber is an excellent stone to keep on hand.

Amber is also a strong stone for helping with stomach problems, all illnesses concerning the bladder, kidneys, liver and throat. Blood diseases are all helped with the use of amber along with any condition involving skin, bones and eyes.

Amethyst

- Strengthens willpower in the treatment of addiction

- Promotes inner strength and balance

- Increases courage

- Stabilizes energy levels

- Improves communication

- Pain relief, especially when concerned with headaches, arthritis and general muscle or bone pain

- Strong stone in the treatment of fibromyalgia and chronic fatigue illnesses

- Strengthens the immune system

- Mood enhancement

- Development of psychic ability

Aventurine
Blue

- Calming

- Balances emotions

- Improves communicative ability

- Enhances creativity and creative thought processes

Green
- Stimulates the imagination
- Enhances positivity
- Improves circulatory issues
- Sleep problems and insomnia
- Headaches

Orange
- Strengthens communications
- Enhances and focuses intellect
- Stimulates feeling of self worth
- Aids imaginative thinking
- Helps to settle and balance the emotions following sexual trauma

Aquamarine
- Increases intuition
- Calms the mind and emotions
- Aids in recovering from all aspects of mental health illness
- Increases self belief and confidence
- Improves communication abilities
- Promotes creative thought processes

Beryl

All color varieties of Beryl are beneficial when dealing with stress related illness and anxiety. It is also helpful when treating illnesses relating to the circulatory system, liver, stomach, spleen, detoxification and the pulmonary processes.

Yellow (Heliodor)

- Improves ability to feel compassion and sympathy
- Increasing understanding of others emotional state
- Promotes healing in all areas affected by the spleen, pancreas and liver
- Strengthens the ability to connect to higher self
- Aids in cleansing of all chakra points

Green

- Increases concentration and stimulates intellect
- Energizing
- Stimulates creative thoughts and actions
- Aids respiratory healing
- Promotes healing in all areas connected to the liver and eyes

Blue

- See Aquamarine

Pink

Promotes empathy
Improves patience and tolerance of others
Aids transition of thought and emotional processes
Enhances the acceptance of self and others
Stimulates calm feelings & love of self and others

White (Clear)
- Strengthens and focuses intellect

- Aids in connection to the wisdom of higher self

- Aids in the expansion of perception

- Helps in the healing of stomach and intestinal disorders

- Detoxifying

- Strengthens self confidence, willpower and mental ability

- Calms and balances the nervous system

- Aids in the healing of spine and bone problems

- Improves conditions relating to stomach ulcers, nausea, depression and eating disorders

Black Tourmaline
- Neutralizing of negative energies

- Calming and grounding excessive nervous energy

- Restraint of obsessive thoughts and behaviors

- Relaxing of fears and emotional instability

- Pain relief in arthritis

- Aids in healing of problems relating to the heart

- Boosts immune system

Bloodstone
- Strengthens courage
- Relieves depression and depressive tendencies
- Detoxifying
- Increases energy levels
- Calms anxiety and nervous tension
- Helps to ease flue, colds, infections and swelling along with all symptoms relating to these conditions
- Focuses thought processes

Blue Quartz
- Strengthens the mind so thought processes become clearer and thoughts are more streamlined
- Improves self discipline
- Reduces fears and anxious thoughts
- Stimulates courage
- Calms hyperactivity and overstimulation
- Helps in healing of the endocrine system

Carnelian
- Promotes feeling of courage and inner strength
- Aids in individual expression of both self and creativity
- Calms emotional instability
- Aids in healing of fevers, colds, hay fever, skin disorders, kidney problems and rheumatism
- Healing for skin conditions

Citrine

- Improves and promotes feelings of self belief and confidence in self

- Strengthens willpower and conviction of thought

- Promotes happiness

- Helps to relieve symptoms of depression

- Settles the mind to encourage rational thought

- Balances mood

- Eases digestive upset

Clear Quartz

Clear Quart is a natural healing crystal and will help in all areas of mental, physical and emotional healing.

- Balances life force energies

Emerald

General all round healing stone which can be used to aid healing through all chakra points.

- Improves respiratory system

- Heart function

- Eyesight

- Circulatory system

- Strengthens spine

- Detoxifying

- Pancreatic and thymus healing

- Improves and strengthens the immune system

- Aids in contact with higher self

Garnet

Garnet is a stone which can be used in the cleansing of each of your chakra points and to aid the balancing of energy flow.

- Increases self awareness and confidence

- Increases the libido

- Calms emotions

- Reduces anger

- Removal of inhibitions

- Promotes healing of the respiratory system, circulatory system and heart, all aspects of blood, spine and bones

Hematite

Reduces fever and temperature
Promotes clearer thought processes
Strengthens logic and problem solving cognitive processes
Balances energy flow
Improves sleep disorders and insomnia
Calms the nervous system
Aids in healing all blood related illness

Jade

- Calms the mind

- Removes negative energies

- Increases ability to remember dreams

- Settles irritability

- Release of stored emotional feelings helping to heal symptoms which have been caused by them

- Stimulates creative and imaginative thought

- Creates feelings of strength of self belief

- Useful in fertility problems

- Strengthens bones and promotes healing in all areas connected to the kidneys and adrenal glands

- Detoxifying

Lapis Lazuli

- Strengthens communicative ability

- Strengthens self belief and confidence in social situations

- Grounds excess nervous energy in both mind and body

- Stimulates kidney and thyroid function

- Aids in the dissipation of stored excess fatty tissue

- Helps to balance the production of hormones through the adrenal gland

- Detoxifying

- Strengthens the link between self and higher self

Orange Calcite

- Lifts the mood and helps to overcome shyness
- Improves depressive thoughts and depression
- Increases sex drive
- Stimulates the imagination
- Strengthens resolve to carry out plans
- Increases confidence and creative and imaginative thought processes

Peridot

- Eases negative emotions
- Calms the nervous system
- Balances emotions
- Strengthens the body's natural healing ability

Pyrite (fool's gold)

- Increases mental ability
- Strengthens and focuses intellect
- Stimulates creativity and imagination
- Improves memory
- Balances the psychological state
- Enhances development of psychic abilities

Red Jasper
- Stabilization of the life force energy

- Calms the mind

- Strengthen control of thought processes

Rose Quartz
- Promotes calmness of mind and emotions

- Increases general happiness and mood

- Strengthens feelings of love of self and others in non selfish ways

Smoky Quartz
- Alleviates depressive thoughts and feelings

- Calms excessive emotions

- Absorbs negative energy

- Settles nervous energy

- Opens the mind to allow access to the subconscious self, (higher self)

- Aids in the healing of conditions relating to the stomach, reproduction, kidneys, water retention and pancreas

- Balances hormone production

Sodalite
- Aids cognitive processes promoting rational thought
- Strengthens communication abilities
- Stimulates intellect
- Promotes focus of mind to enhance ability to learn and recall
- Aids with sleep disorders and insomnia
- Strengthens healing of colds and flu
- Settles digestive disorders

Tigers Eye
- Strengthens practical thought processes
- Clears mental vision
- Strengthens willpower
- Calms ailments relating to the stomach
- Settles and balances the emotions

Tourmaline
All varieties of tourmaline help with the enhancement of mood and aid in the strengthening of self belief and confidence. They are also useful in the treatment of any ailment connected to the lymphatic system.
Blue
- Improves communication and speech
- Reduction in mental tension
- Aids in healing of thyroid problems and ailments of the throat

Pink

- Balances the emotions
- Promotes understanding and acceptance of self
- Transforms negative thoughts and emotions into positive ones
- Calming
- Improves strength of mind

Black & Green

- Regulates and balance blood pressure
- Reduces symptoms of stress and calms the nervous system.

Turquoise

- Turquoise is a healing stone which promotes full mind and body healing
- Strengthens communication
- Boosts the immune system
- Improves respiratory problems
- Strengthens healing in all areas jointly governed by the heart & throat chakras

Conclusion

Thank you again for buying this book!

I hope this book contained enough information to help you to understand and use crystals and minerals for their therapeutic benefits. My aim was to show you how simple the practice of natural healing is and how easily you can benefit from it.

The next step is to purchase some healing crystals and minerals for yourself and spend some time familiarizing yourself with them. Learn to recognize the different stones and become familiar with how their individual energies feel so you can build the confidence to try crystal healing for yourself.

Practice cleansing and energizing your stones then invite friends and family over and practice your healing techniques with them. Before you know it you will be using expanding your knowledge of the stones and reaping the rewards of natural healing.

Finally, if you enjoyed this book, please take the time to share your thoughts and post a review on Amazon. It'd be greatly appreciated!

Thank you and good luck!

Made in the USA
Las Vegas, NV
09 November 2021